STAR ✪ FILES

Usher

Dan Whitcombe

www.raintreepublishers.co.uk

Visit our website to find out more information about **Raintree** books.

To order:
☎ Phone 44 (0) 1865 888113
▤ Send a fax to 44 (0) 1865 314091
▱ Visit the Raintree Bookshop at **www.raintreepublishers.co.uk** to browse our catalogue and order online.

Produced for Raintree by
White-Thomson Publishing Ltd
Bridgewater Business Centre
210 High Street, Lewes, BN7 2NH

First published in Great Britain by Raintree,
Halley Court, Jordan Hill, Oxford OX2 8EJ,
part of Harcourt Education.
Raintree is a registered trademark
of Harcourt Education Ltd.

Editorial: Nicola Hodgson,
Sarah Shannon, and Kate Buckingham
Design: Tinstar Design Ltd (www.tinstar.co.uk)
and Michelle Lisseter
Picture Research: Nicola Hodgson
Production: Chloe Bloom

Originated by Modern Age
Printed and bound in China by
South China Printing Company

ISBN 1 844 43298 X
09 08 07 06 05
10 9 8 7 6 5 4 3 2 1

**British Library Cataloguing
in Publication Data**
Dan Whitcombe.
Usher. – (Star Files)
782.4'21643'092

A full catalogue record for this book
is available from the British Library.

Acknowledgements
The publishers would like to thank the following
for permission to reproduce photographs: Allstar
Picture Library pp. **17** (l), **43** (l), **43** (r); Corbis
pp. **4** (Laura Farr/ZUMA), **12** (t); Getty Images
pp. **9** (b), **11** (l) (Frank Micelotta), **12** (b)
(Frank Micelotta), **32** (Frank Micelotta), **35**
(Dave Hogan), **40** (Frank Micelotta); Retna
Pictures Ltd pp. **5** (Mitchell Layton), **7** (l)
(Sara De Boer), **10** (Darla Khazei), **11** (r)
(Alex Treacher), **13** (Tara Canova), **15** (John
Spellman),**16** (Photofest), **19** (l) (Darla Khazei),
20 (Gregorio Binuya), **24** (Sara De Boer), **25**
(Heungman), **28** (John Spellman), **29** (Debbie
Smyth), **33** (Grayson Alexander), **37** (Carmen
Valdes); Rex Features pp. **6** (JC), **7** (r) (Camilla
Morandi), **8** (Everett Collection), **9** (t)
(S Gaboury/DMI), **14** (STK), **17** (r) (Ken McKay),
19 (r) (Dave Lewis), **21** (l) (Brian Rasic), **21** (r)
(Ken McKay), **22** (Chapman/ACP), **23** (Sipa
Press), **26** (Action Press), **27** (l) (Matt Baron/BEI),
27 (r) (Charles Sykes), **30** (I.B.L.), **31** (Action
Press), **34** (Charles Sykes), **36** (l) (I.B.L.), **36** (r)
(Action Press), **38** (WJO), **39** (LXL), **41** (Action
Press), **42** (Sipa Press). Cover photograph
reproduced with permission of Corbis.

Quote sources: pp. **5**, **13**, **19**, **33** mtv.com; pp. **6**,
8 (b) mtvnews.com; p. **8** (t) www.usherworld.com,
pp. **18**, **21** *Star Tribune*, 5 September 2004; pp. **20**,
28 FunkyUsher.homestead.com; p. **22** *The Sun*, 19
March 2004; p. **24** *Daily Mirror*, 24 August 2004;
p. **26** www.teenmusic.com; p. **31** MTV Q&A
interview, 2004; p. **39** www.femalefirst.co.uk;
p. **40** *Usher: The Ultimate Entertainer*, by Marc
Malkin; p. **42** www.ottawasun.com

The publishers would like to thank Sarah
Williams, Charly Rimsa, Rosie Nixon, Catherine
Clarke, and Caroline Hamilton for their assistance
in the preparation of this book.

Every effort has been made to contact the
copyright holders of any material reproduced
in this book. Any omissions will be rectified
in subsequent printings if notice is given to
the publishers.

The paper used to print this book comes
from sustainable resources.

Disclaimer: This book is not authorized
or approved by Usher.

Contents

Any words appearing in the text in bold, **like this**, are explained in the glossary. You can also look out for them in the Star words box at the bottom of each page.

Global superstar

Usher is now a top star in the music world. "He's a little Elvis right now." That is how popular singer Brandy described Usher after his song "Yeah!" became a huge hit in 2004. This is pretty remarkable for someone who started out singing in a choir in a small town in Tennessee.

Star from the start

Usher has always been clear about what he wanted to achieve. Even when he was a young kid, he knew he wanted to be a star. He was spotted by a music **executive** at a talent show when he was just 14 years old. Within a year he had moved to New York and was making music with rap star Sean Combs.

ALL ABOUT USHER

Full name: Usher Raymond IV
Born: 14 October 1978
Place of birth: Dallas, Texas, USA
Family: Usher Raymond III (father), Jonetta Patton (mother), James (brother)
Height: 5 feet 9½ inches (1.75 metres)
Marital status: single
Big break: Offered a **recording contract** with the LaFace record label after being spotted at a talent show
Other interests: American football, basketball, fashion, fitness

Star words

producer (in music) music producers decide how a song will sound when it is being recorded

Number one

When his album *Confessions* came out in 2004, Usher became one of the most successful music stars of all time. He has number one records and the respect of the music industry. In the future, he is likely to have even greater successes waiting for him in the world of music and film.

66 *Strivers achieve what dreamers believe.* 99

Find out later

Who was one of the **producers** on Usher's first album?

Which member of girlband TLC did Usher date for 2 years?

Who is Usher's biggest rival?

Usher is always an exciting live performer.

recording contract agreement between a musician and a record label to make music together

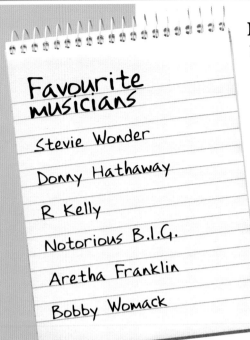

Favourite musicians

Stevie Wonder

Donny Hathaway

R Kelly

Notorious B.I.G.

Aretha Franklin

Bobby Womack

Stevie Wonder is one of Usher's musical heroes.

Family values

Usher was born in Dallas, Texas, United States, on 14 October 1978. However, his mum and dad did not get on. Usher's mother Jonetta moved with her son to Chattanooga, Tennessee, when Usher was 1 year old.

Musical roots

Usher grew up in Chattanooga with his younger brother, James. He was always involved in music. His mum led the choir of the local church, St Elmo's Missionary Baptist Church. Usher liked playing sports when he was young, but his main love was singing. He sang solos in the church choir when he was small. He also liked acting. He wanted to be a star. His mother supported him in his wish. He took part in talent shows. Jonetta also encouraged him to **audition** for television adverts. Usher always wanted to act as well as sing.

Centre of attention

Even when he was a small child, Usher was always the centre of attention. As his mother explains: "When he was young, we made a big deal out of birthday parties. When other people's kids had birthday parties, he thought it was his birthday party too, and got really mad because he wanted to be the centre of attention."

Star words   audition interview for an actor or musician, where they show their skills

Mother and manager

Usher did not have much contact with his father after he and his mother moved to Chattanooga. He was very close to his mum, though. She became very involved in his musical career. She is still Usher's **manager**. She also runs her own company, called J-Pat Management. This company looks after pop stars.

Usher is known as one of the most stylish performers around.

Usher's style

Usher has always had a strong sense of style. When he was small, his mum used to plait his long hair. Usher did not like her doing this. He secretly had his long hair cut off. He then refused to tell his mum who had done it.

Usher's mum, Jonetta, is also his manager.

manager music managers take care of the business side of a pop star's career

Soul stars

Usher loves soul singers. He says that singers such as Al Green and Stevie Wonder have been very important to him. Usher's grandparents were big fans of the soul singer Marvin Gaye (below). They played Gaye's music to him from an early age.

Opening act

By the time Usher was 12 years old, his experience singing in church had proved that he had a great voice. He had also shown how serious he was about being a star. He had already been in a few local talent shows. He had also been to **auditions** for television adverts. Usher's first experience of being a pop star came when he joined a local band called NuBeginnings. There were five boys in the band. They performed at local shows, and even made an album, called *NuBeginning*. Usher felt he had taken his first step towards becoming a star.

> ❝ It was all about the music. It's my biggest passion and my biggest joy. ❞

Change of scene

Usher thought that NuBeginnings was perfect for him, but Jonetta had other ideas for her son. After 3 months, she took him out of the band. This did not make her popular with Usher. "He told me I had destroyed his whole life", she remembers.

★ Star fact

Usher's favourite sports team is the Atlanta Hawks basketball team.

Star words   Motown record label that released popular music by African-American singers in the 1960s

New beginning

In 1991, when Usher was thirteen, Jonetta moved the family to Atlanta, Georgia. Atlanta is one of the most famous musical cities in the United States. Many of the biggest stars of soul, pop, R&B, rap, and hip-hop came out of Atlanta. Usher just had to hope that some of their success would rub off on him.

Usher moved to the city of Atlanta when he was 13 years old.

Hitting the high notes

Star Search

In 1991, Usher won Best Teen Vocalist on *Star Search*. This is a television talent show in the United States. It is a good way for young singers to get their first break. Many other singers have also appeared on *Star Search*. These include Britney Spears, Christina Aguilera, and Justin Timberlake.

Usher was very angry about being taken out of NuBeginnings. However, he soon realized that he should trust his mother. Atlanta gave him many more chances to make his dreams of stardom come true.

Making waves

When he was in Atlanta, Usher started to go to more talent shows than ever before. At one show he was spotted by a **talent scout** called A. J. Alexander. He also impressed a record label **executive**. This led to an **audition** for one of the most important men in music, Antonio "L. A." Reid. He was one of the people in charge of LaFace Records.

L. A. Reid is behind some of the biggest musical talents in Atlanta – including Usher.

Star words

rumour story that lots of people discuss, but that may not be true

Usher and P. Diddy still perform together sometimes, more than 10 years after their first meeting.

It was a huge deal for Usher to be signed to LaFace records. It is a very well respected record label. It has been the home to many top music stars, including Outkast, Pink (below), TLC, and Toni Braxton.

Waiting game

According to **rumours**, Reid signed Usher to a **recording contract** on the spot. That was in 1992, when Usher was fourteen. However, making it in music often takes a long time. Usher recorded the song "Call me a Mack" for the **soundtrack** of the 1993 film *Poetic Justice*. Shortly after that, his voice broke. This meant that he lost his **unique** singing voice. LaFace nearly dropped him from the label.

★ Star fact

Poetic Justice starred singer Janet Jackson and rapper Tupac Shakur.

Sean Combs

Luckily for Usher, he was spotted by the singer and **producer** Sean Combs, who was also known as P. Diddy. Sean offered to take Usher to New York to help him develop a new, more grown-up, image. Usher had to be patient. In the end, it took 2 years from being spotted until he recorded his first album in 1994, when he was 16.

talent scout someone who looks out for talented performers such as actors, models, or athletes

Big city life

Living in New York was a big move for Usher. Although Sean Combs was looking after him, and his mother also took care of him, he was still a 15-year-old boy living in a very big city.

Usher did not write the songs for his **debut** album, *Usher*. He did not have any say in the way that the music sounded, either. This meant he was not really in control of the music he put his name to. He felt unsatisfied with this. Sean Combs helped to **produce** his first album. He also tried to help Usher with his image. Combs' ideas for Usher were a bit grown-up for a 15-year-old boy, though. He thought Usher should have a "bad-boy" image. This caused problems between them.

Usher moved to New York to start his life in music.

Sean Combs

Sean Combs was a huge R&B and hip-hop star himself. He had set up his own label, Bad Boy Entertainment, in 1993. This released work by artists such as Notorious B.I.G. and Faith Evans. Sean is a famous record producer, too. He is also known for his popular clothing line, Sean John.

Sean Combs had a big part to play in Usher's debut album.

Star words   collaborate work together with

First releases

The whole experience was a lot for Usher to take in. This was especially true after his first single, "Thinking of You", was released in 1995. This was the first time that Usher was really in the public eye. After the single came out, the album *Usher* was released. It sold 250,000 copies across the United States. This was not quite as big a success as Usher had wanted. However, he was now on the edge of pop stardom.

66 *Where I come from and how I was raised was to really understand music.* 99

Teaming up

Although Usher was a solo artist, that does not mean he always worked alone. By 1995 he had already **collaborated** with other singers. He also made songs for film **soundtracks**. He joined other R&B singers, including D'Angelo, to record the single "You Will Know". This featured on the soundtrack to the 1994 film *Jason's Lyric*. He also teamed up with R&B singer Monica for the duet "Let's Straighten it Out".

Making a record

Making a record is a complicated process. Usher worked with a team of songwriters who wrote the songs. Then he worked with producers who came into the studio to create the sound heard on the record. The producers and songwriters were employed by the record label. This means that it was really LaFace who decided what *Usher* would sound like.

Singer D'Angelo was one of the first musicians that Usher teamed up with.

Taking control

Number two

"You Make Me Wanna" could have been a number one record. However, another song, Elton John's "Candle in the Wind", was released at the same time. This song was a **tribute** to Diana, Princess of Wales. She had recently died in a tragic car accident. The song became one of the best-selling singles of all time.

Selling 250,000 copies of your **debut** album sounds pretty good. However, LaFace had hoped for more from their new star. Usher himself was unhappy with his work with Sean Combs. He left New York and went back to Atlanta. For his second album, Usher wanted to have more control. He wanted to decide what kind of music he was making. To do that, he had to write the songs himself! Usher co-wrote six of the nine songs for his second album, *My Way*. This came out in 1997.

Star fact

Between making *Usher* and *My Way*, Usher went back to graduate from high school.

Usher was pleased with the results of his second album.

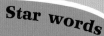
Star words

14

nominated put forward as one of the right people to win an award

Jermaine Dupri helped Usher to develop a new sound for his second album, *My Way*.

Teamwork

This time, Usher chose who he worked with. He had a team of songwriters he respected. They included Jermaine Dupri, Babyface, and Teddy Riley. They all had years of experience. Usher spent 6 months living at Dupri's house in Atlanta while he recorded the album.

Going global

The results of this teamwork were impressive. The first single from the album was called "You Make Me Wanna". It was a number two hit on the pop charts. The album sold 7 million copies across the world. The next single, "Nice & Slow", was Usher's first pop number one. It was not just the fans who were impressed. Usher won a Soul Train Award for pop. He was also **nominated** for a Grammy award for one song on the album. The Grammy awards are the most important music awards in the United States.

Grammy bloop

As well as being nominated for a Grammy, Usher was now famous enough to be asked to present an award at the ceremony. Usher must have been nervous. When he presented the Album of the Year award to legendary musician Bob Dylan, he called him "Bill"!

tribute act that shows feelings of respect or admiration towards someone

Moesha

From 1996 until 2001, *Moesha* was one of the United States' most popular television programmes. It followed the lives of a group of teenage friends and their families. When Usher starred in the programme, from 1997 to 1998, he played a character called Jeremy. He was the boyfriend of Moesha, the girl who gave her name to the show. Moesha was played by R&B singer Brandy.

Screen tests

Usher always had a lot of goals. He did not just want to be a popular singer and songwriter. He also wanted to be a star of television and cinema. From 1997, when he was nineteen, Usher started to become known as an actor and television star. He appeared on television programmes such as *Moesha*. He also went on chat shows such as *Oprah*.

Singer Brandy played the lead role of Moesha. The cast also included Lamont Bentley, William Allen Young, and Marcus T. Paulk.

Star words

cameo when a famous person has a small part in a film or television programme

Usher acted with Rosario Dawson in *Light It Up*.

Life on film

In 1998, Usher had a **cameo** as a DJ in the comedy horror film *The Faculty*. The following year he appeared in the film *Light It Up*. This was a drama about a group of teenagers who try to improve their school.

★ Star fact

Usher was very pleased to appear on the television programme *The Bold and the Beautiful* in 1998. It is his mum's favourite soap opera.

Usher was one of the hottest young stars of 1998.

Live action

In 1998, Usher was so busy with his television and film projects that he did not have time to record any new musical material. To keep his fans happy, he released a live album of **medleys** and previous hits recorded while he was touring.

medley song that mixes parts of a number of songs together

17

Superstar status

The release of *My Way* really put Usher on the map. By 1999, Usher was one of the hottest young stars around. This was what he had always dreamed of. In 1998–1999, Usher also toured with one of his heroes, Janet Jackson. He made sure he was noticed during this tour. He was Jackson's support act, so he only had 15 minutes on stage. He still managed to fit in almost as many costume changes as she did for her full 2-hour show.

Media star

Usher had always said that his aim was to become "Mr Entertainment". He was appearing in films and on television. He spent months touring. He went to award ceremonies, where he often presented awards to other artists. He says, "Being an ultimate entertainer is not just about being a stage performer. It's about being an actor; it's about being a **producer**; it's about being a **director**."

Touring the country

Usher was the opening act for Janet Jackson's 1998 Velvet Rope tour when it started in Washington DC. Then, before *My Way* was released, Usher toured the whole country. He performed "Back-to-School" concerts at high schools and Boys and Girls Clubs in almost every state in the United States.

Star fact

Usher is a big fan of the "bling" lifestyle. He has even admitted that he has honey flown in from Paris, France, for his breakfast!

Love duet

The press were interested in Usher's music. They were even more interested in his private life, however. In 2001, he started to attract attention because he was dating another music star. She was Rozonda "Chilli" Thomas, of the band TLC.

Star words   director person in charge of making a film

The fact that they were both in the music business helped them understand each other. He said, "When it comes to work, we understand each other, we respect each other. I'm supportive of her, she's supportive of me. That's what real friendship is about."

Usher and Chilli were one of the hottest couples in R&B.

TLC

TLC (above) was one of the biggest R&B and hip-hop bands of the late 1990s. The three girls in the band were Rozonda, Tionne "T-Boz" Watkins, and Lisa "Left Eye" Lopes. Their biggest album was 1999's *FanMail*. It included one of their most famous songs, "No Scrubs". Sadly, Lisa Lopes was killed in a car accident in 2002.

19

Dancer

Usher is almost as well known for his dance moves as he is for his songs. He is one of the fittest performers around. He often impresses his audience by doing handstands and backflips during a song.

Working it

Making public appearances, recording music, and being in television all sound like fun. It was also hard work for Usher, though. He was one of the hardest working pop stars around. He had little time for himself. This meant he did not have much time for Chilli, either. He says, "One of the reasons I have not been able to get into a serious relationship is that I work so much. I know it's a sacrifice to put my **career** first, but it means putting love on the shelf and being lonely by myself."

Non-stop routine

Success always comes at a price. For Usher, being a big star after *My Way* meant that the offers of work kept coming in. *My Way* was an international success, which Usher's first album had not been. This meant that Usher could tour all around the world. For Usher, singing live on stage was one of the most important parts of being a star.

Singing live has always been important to Usher.

Star words   career what someone does for a job

Keeping up the pace

Usher is famous for his physical fitness and his amazing dance routines. He spends hours in the gym to keep fit. Once, he said that he had sit-up competitions with his backing dancers. He claimed that his record was more than 1000. He says, "When I'm touring, I … keep my physique together from the [stage] sweat. However, I have a crew that works all the time doing crunches, competing against each other."

Usher hangs out with one of his favourite designers, Giorgio Armani.

Not many pop stars can do moves like this!

21

R&B

R&B stands for Rhythm and Blues. Originally, R&B was a form of African-American music that influenced rock 'n' roll in the 1950s. It became even more important in the 1960s, with the birth of soul and funk. Artists who have been **inspired** by R&B include Prince and R Kelly in the 1980s and 1990s, as well as legends such as Ray Charles, Aretha Franklin (right), and Sam Cooke from the 1950s through to the 1970s.

Time to reflect

There was a gap of 4 years between *My Way* and Usher's next major album, *8701*, which came out in 2001. In that time, he spent months touring live. He also appeared in films and on television and became a huge pop star with a famous girlfriend. For Usher, it was not the glamour and the fame that was the most important thing in his life. It was still the music.

Only the best will do

Usher was not happy to become a legend just because he appeared on the front cover of magazines. He had spent many long hours working to become one of R&B's most impressive live performers. He needed to be just as professional in the recording studio.

When Usher made *8701*, he wanted to have the best people working with him. His live act depended on the best **choreographers** around.

> I want to help develop R&B all over the world. That's my mission.

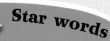

Star words

choreographer person who makes up dance steps and teaches them to others

In the same way, his next album would be a **collaboration** with the best **producers**, the best writers, and the best pop video **directors**.

Musical mission

Usher felt that his fame and wealth also meant that he had a duty. He felt he had a responsibility to serve R&B. He wanted to make the best R&B music he could, and make sure that the world took notice.

Usher's soundtracks

Usher's songs have appeared in these films:

Paid in Full (2002)

The Sweetest Thing (2002)

Soul Food (1997)

Kazaam (1996)

Panther (1995)

Jason's Lyric (1994)

Poetic Justice (1993)

By 2001, Usher had worked hard to become a great live performer.

inspired take ideas from something

Style and image

★ ★ ★ ★ ★ ★ ★ ★ ★

Celebrations

Usher's mum wanted to celebrate Usher's being **nominated** at the MTV Video Music Awards in 2004. She hired a luxury 146-foot yacht to host a "Welcome to Miami" party for her son's show business friends. Famous people who came to the party included Christina Aguilera, basketball player Shaquille O'Neal, and music stars the Neptunes.

★ ★ ★ ★ ★ ★ ★ ★

Image is one of the most important things for any superstar. Sometimes, one style is not enough for a whole **career** in music. Just think of Madonna. She is almost as famous for changing her image as she is for selling records.

> I wear expensive jewellery, drive a big car, and when I feel like treating myself to something, I do it.

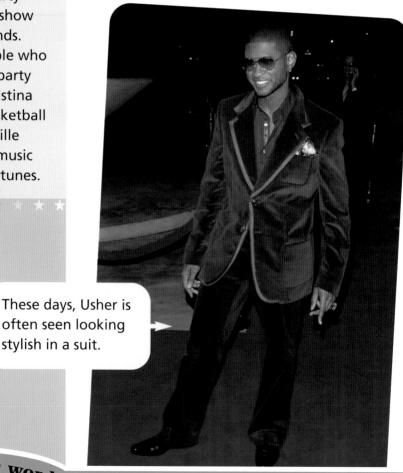

These days, Usher is often seen looking stylish in a suit.

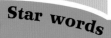

Star words   medallion type of necklace

Young gun

In the early days, Usher could always be recognized by his headwear. He was often seen wearing a baseball cap or tight elastic hat. Until the release of his second album, Usher did not feel confident about his looks. When he was sixteen, like many teenagers, he suffered from acne. He was not yet the athlete he would become as he got older. On the front cover of his first album, Usher hides his body under big jumpers and baggy jackets.

Fitness first

By the time of the release of *My Way*, the hard work of performing live had made Usher one of the fittest singers around. This also meant that his look changed. He would often wear vests and open shirts over low-slung baggy trousers. He was often seen wearing a "U" **medallion** set with diamonds. However, not everything changed. Usher still loved to wear hats!

Usher's U-shaped medallion is a favourite item.

Public property

Being a big star has its advantages. Usher can go anywhere he wants and stay in the best hotels. He can buy himself expensive cars and designer clothes. He can go to the best restaurants and nightclubs. There is always a price for fame, however. Although Usher is very grateful for his success, being in the public eye means that he has very little time for himself.

Bodyguards

Things are tough at the top. At one point Usher even had to hire a bodyguard to keep autograph hunters at bay. As he says: "It's hard because people get angry at you, but I've got a life to live too."

Usher spends time signing autographs for the fans who helped him to become so successful.

Star words   hectic very busy

Now Usher is so successful he often has a bodyguard with him.

Spend, spend, spend

It can be hard to be in the public eye all the time. However, being a rich and famous pop star has its advantages. Usher loves to buy clothes. He has admitted to spending US$7,500 on a single pair of trousers!

Usher dresses like the millionaire he is.

A hectic life

Success can be difficult. The more popular Usher becomes, the more **hectic** his life is. It might sound like fun, but touring across the world can also be very tiring. Especially when you also have to find time to record new songs, appear on television, and attend award ceremonies. Even as early as *My Way*, Usher's life was very busy. He had only one day to learn all the dance moves for the first single from the album, "You Make Me Wanna".

All about the music

The Grammy awards

The Grammy awards are the United States' biggest music awards. The ceremony is usually held in Los Angeles, and sometimes in New York. It is shown on television across the world. One of the best things about the awards is that they are given to musicians for their talent and **accomplishments,** not just for the number of records they have sold.

Usher had sold millions of records by 2001. However, that year he released his album *8701*. This was the start of something new for him. Before the album came out, Usher was considered to be a "teen" pop star rather than a serious R&B artist. That was all about to change.

> " I wanted to make an album with songs that could appeal to everyone. "

Usher celebrates the release of his third album, *8701*, in 2001.

The A team

For his first "serious" R&B album, Usher worked with some of the best names in music. His **producers** included Edmund "Eddie Hustle" Clement. He also worked with Jermaine Dupri again. Dupri even sang on some of the songs. Other people that Usher worked with included Jimmy Jam, Terry Lewis, and, most importantly, the Neptunes. Chad Hugo and Pharrell Williams helped Usher to develop a harder, more sophisticated sound.

Getting recognized

It is one thing to get recognized on red carpets around the world or to appear on television chat shows. Now Usher wanted to get **credit** for his music within the industry itself. This meant both high sales and music awards. *My Way* had won Usher two Billboard Music awards. However, Usher won his first Grammy for his work on *8701*. This was for the single, "U Remind Me", which was named Best R&B Vocal Performance. The album also sold very well. It went eight-times platinum. This meant that it sold more than 8 million copies.

The Neptunes

Pharrell Williams (below) and Chad Hugo are two of the hottest names in music. They are producers and songwriters. They have produced songs for pop acts such as Britney Spears and Justin Timberlake, as well as hip-hop stars including LL Cool J and Busta Rhymes. They also make their own music, under the names N.E.R.D and the Neptunes.

Confessions

Recording your
personal feelings
is something you
have to be very
careful about.
This explains why
the release of
Confessions took
so long. It was
supposed to come
out in November
2003, but Usher
felt it was not
quite right. He
had recorded
more than 40
songs. In the end,
the album was not
released until
March 2004.

All in the preparation

There was a long gap between *Usher* and *My Way*.
Usher fans also had a long wait between *My Way*
and *8701*. Patience is no bad thing, however. Each
album was better than the one before. It was in the
3 years between *8701* in 2001 and *Confessions* in
2004 that Usher learnt the most.

Getting personal

8701 was a great R&B album. Usher had
become one of the best singers around. His live
performances were **sensational**. The production
and songwriting were also better than on *My Way*.
When he made *Confessions*, Usher used a lot of his
personal life experiences. His life in 2003 had been
complicated. He had been going out with
Chilli Thomas for 2 years. There were
rumours in the **media** that the couple
would soon get married. However,
life in the public eye can be difficult.
Many famous couples have suffered
from media attention. Usher
and Chilli found
this out, too.

Usher had serious things
to sing about in 2004.

Star words

media types of communication such as television, radio,
newspapers, and magazines

Heart to heart

It soon became clear that Chilli and Usher were not happy. Some people said that Usher had been dating someone else. Neither Usher nor Chilli talked to the press about their relationship. However, they split up before the album was released. In many ways, *Confessions* is a diary of the singer's regrets and sadness at losing Chilli.

> "I've got a lot to say. I've got a lot of stuff built in me that I just want to let go of."

Having a lot of attention from the media put pressure on Usher and Chilli.

First single

Part of the problem with a new album is deciding which is going to be the first single from it. Normally, the first single is released before the album itself. It tells fans what the rest of the album is going to sound like. With *Confessions*, the song "Yeah!" was the first single. It was R&B mixed with dance. This was a sound that worked both on the radio and in nightclubs.

sensational very exciting and impressive

Top ten

In 2004, Usher became only the third artist to have three singles in the US Billboard Top Ten at the same time. "Burn" was at number one. "Yeah!" was at number four. "Confessions PtII" was at number nine. The only other acts to have done this are the Beatles and the Bee Gees.

Private vs public

Confessions was an album with a difference. It was a very personal and honest album, with a **confessional** tone. Usher used music to tell the world what was going on in his life. This led him to have his most amazing public and professional success.

Record breaking

Some of Usher's favourite musicians, including Jermaine Dupri and the Neptunes, worked on *Confessions*. This meant that the album would not disappoint Usher's fans. However, the success of the first single, "Yeah!", took everyone by surprise. *Confessions* went straight into the US Billboard charts at number one. It was also number one in the UK. It sold an amazing 1.1 million records in its first week. This was a world record for an R&B album. The album sold an incredible 5 million copies in the first 6 months.

Usher with one of the few copies of *Confessions* that had not already sold!

Star words

confessional book, film, or piece of music that tells a true personal story

Usher goes home with another armful of awards from the Billboard Music Awards in 2004.

Awards

Usher won more awards for *Confessions* than we have space to mention. He was **nominated** for four American Music Awards. He was named Best Male Artist at the World Music Awards. At the MTV video awards, "Yeah!" won the Best Male Video and Best Dance Video.

Gaining respect

Confessions sold a lot of copies and won a lot of awards. It also brought Usher respect in the music business. Usher appeared on the front of magazines such as *Rolling Stone* and *Vibe*. These are serious music magazines. Their front covers are given to the biggest artists in the world of music.

"This album is my chance to be real."

Laser works

X is one of the most respected music video directors. He is most famous for his work with artists such as Nelly (below), Kanye West, R Kelly, and Beenie Man. He has also filmed television adverts.

Sound and vision

Although Usher is most interested in the way his music sounds, he knows that image is very important, too. His live shows include special effects, amazing dancing, and lots of costume changes. He also makes sure his music videos are the best around. A great video is almost as important as a great song.

X-Factor

The single "Yeah!" was a perfect introduction to the album *Confessions*. It was a number one song in the US Billboard Charts. People were already talking about it before the record was released. This is because the video was already playing on television. The video was one of Usher's best ever. It was the work of a **director** called X, formerly known as Little X. His work with special effects lasers gave the video a great look.

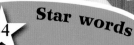

comparison when people see similarities between things

X filmed Usher doing his famous dance moves in front of hundreds of blue and green laser beams. The lights shift and rotate with the song's beat.

Film music

The video was filmed over 2 days in an empty art gallery in Los Angeles. First of all, Usher had to choose dancers to appear with him. Then a dance floor was built in the gallery. **Choreographers** came in to work on the dance moves with Usher and his 40 back-up dancers.

"Yeah!" won Best Male Video at the MTV Video Music Awards in 2004. Usher accepted the award from Sean Combs, Ludacris, and Lil Jon.

Michael Jackson

The lasers and Usher's smooth dancing led to **comparisons** with Michael Jackson's video for "Rock With You". Jackson has made some of the greatest videos of all time. His 1980s hits "Thriller" and "Bad" are still examples of how to make a great pop video today.

Teamwork

Ever since leaving NuBeginnings, Usher has concentrated on being a solo artist. After his first album, he has also tried to be in control. He is involved with writing his songs and creating his videos. He comes up with new dance moves. Being a solo artist and having artistic control does not mean working alone, however. Every one of Usher's songs, live shows, and videos are a team effort. He works hard with video artists, **choreographers**, dancers, **producers**, and songwriters.

A night for Ray Charles

In October 2004 Usher appeared in a **tribute** concert to legendary musician Ray Charles (above), who had died in June. Usher was joined by Stevie Wonder, Mary J. Blige, and Elton John.

Pairing up

Usher also works with other solo artists. Often, other singers appear on his albums. Usher has also performed on albums of musicians that he respects. In 2004, he starred in Beyoncé Knowles' video for "Naughty Girl". The same year he did a duet with Alicia Keys for "My Boo". Meanwhile, Lil' Kim provided guest vocals for "Just Like Me" from *My Way*.

Alicia Keys is just one of the talented singers Usher has worked with.

Even P. Diddy has appeared on an Usher album. He sang on "I Don't Know" from *8701*. Usher has also been a guest vocalist on Lil Jon's album *Crunk Juice*.

On the road together

Right from the earliest years, Usher toured with some of the biggest names in R&B. Some of the people he toured with include two of his biggest heroines, Janet Jackson and Mary J. Blige. He also supported P. Diddy on his No Way Out tour.

Usher joins forces with rapper Lil Jon.

Famous duets

There have been famous **collaborations** all through the history of popular music. Michael Jackson and Paul McCartney duetted in the 1980s, as did George Michael and soul legend Aretha Franklin. Paul McCartney has also worked with Usher's hero, Stevie Wonder. Of course, often two young stars get together too, like Justin Timberlake and Nelly.

37

Justin Timberlake

Justin Timberlake first found fame on television when he was just a child. He was a television presenter on a programme called the *Mickey Mouse Club*. He then became one of the five members of 'NSYNC. Their album, *No Strings Attached* (2000) became the fastest selling album of all time. Now Justin has had huge success as a solo artist.

Stiff competition

Usher has always been open about the people he admires in the music world. He has always been keen to work with the best people around. However, life at the top is full of **rivalries**. There are many artists who would like to be thought of as the top star in R&B. The **media** is often more interested in trying to find **feuds** than in reporting when artists work together on a project.

It's Justin time

Perhaps the most famous of Usher's rivals has been Justin Timberlake. Like Usher, he started in a boyband. However, Justin actually became famous while he was still in the multi-million record-selling group, 'NSYNC. The rivalry really began when Justin went solo. His **debut** solo album, *Justified* (2003), was a modern style of dance and R&B. In many ways this was similar to the sort of music Usher was making with *8701* and *Confessions*.

Justin shows off his own dance routines.

Star words

feud argument or disagreement

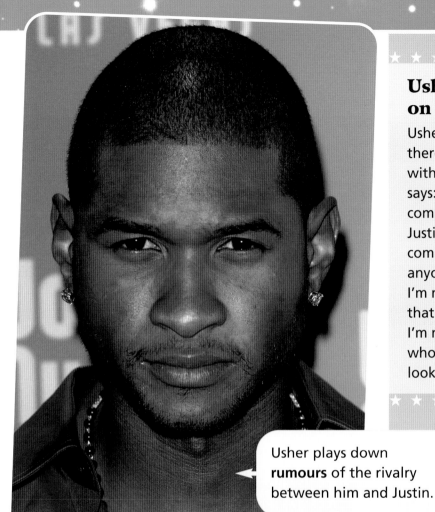

Usher on Justin

Usher now denies there is any feud, with Justin. He says: "I'm not in competition with Justin. I'm not in competition with anyone but myself. I'm not looking for that bad-boy image, I'm not a person who goes out looking for trouble."

★ ★ ★ ★ ★ ★ ★ ★ ★ ★

Usher plays down **rumours** of the rivalry between him and Justin.

Similarities

Usher and Justin have many things in common. Both are managed by their mothers. Both have worked with the Neptunes, and both have toured with P. Diddy. They are also huge sex symbols in the music business. They are even rivals when it comes to acting. Usher has appeared in several films. Justin is working on a number of projects, including the film *Edison*.

Where from here?

iTunes chart

In June 2004 the single "Yeah!" went to number one in the first ever iTunes chart. This is the chart of singles "bought" through Apple's MP3 music library.

There is no doubt that Usher has come a long way since he left Chattanooga. The journey from choirboy to worldwide superstar has not been an easy one. Usher has worked hard for his success. He continues to set himself new targets. Let us just think about what he has already achieved.

> I've accomplished a lot of things already. But I still have my whole life ahead of me, and more to do.

Sales and figures

Usher's 2004 album *Confessions* was the highlight of his career. It was the seventh-fastest selling album of all time. It sold 1.1 million copies in the first week, and gave him three top ten hits in the same week. It was so popular that Usher released a Special Edition of the album in October 2004. This included four extra songs. One of these, a duet with Alicia Keys called "My Boo", gave Usher his fourth number one single of the year. Usher is now a truly global superstar. He has sold more than 40 million records.

Usher brought out a Special Edition of *Confessions*.

SPECIAL EDITION

FEATURES
• 4 New tracks

He has worked with the biggest stars in the world, from Janet Jackson and Beyoncé Knowles to the Neptunes.

Multi-media

It is not all about the music. Usher was first spotted on television, on the *Star Search* talent show. He started out with appearances on shows such as *Moesha* and *Oprah*. He then went on to have **cameo** parts in films including *The Faculty*. We are likely to be seeing more of Usher on screen soon.

Sales

By the end of 2004, *Confessions*, including the Special Edition of the album, had sold 10 million copies worldwide. This was a great achievement for Usher.

Usher celebrates the first million sales of *Confessions*.

Usher on the future

Usher says, "I don't plan on retiring any time soon, I'm just getting warmed up. As a stage performer I feel like I'm at the top of my game ... I don't think I'll ever stop trying to be the ultimate entertainer because there will always be a new obstacle in entertainment."

Star quality

Many people would be happy to achieve what Usher has achieved at so young an age. However, these days many music stars are not content with just having a number one hit. Eminem is a typical example. Although he is most famous for his hip-hop albums, he has also gone into films, acting in the movie *8 Mile*. Beyoncé is another musician who has also appeared in films.

Other **crossover artists** include Jennifer Lopez, Will Smith, and Justin Timberlake. This is nothing new. Top artists have always looked for new challenges. Elvis Presley made a number of films, as have Prince and Madonna.

Usher has plenty to smile about – including his plans for the future.

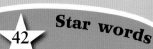

crossover artist when a star who is famous for one thing, such as music, starts to do something new, such as acting

Film projects

Usher is now taking more creative control of his screen appearances. One of the many projects he has been linked with is *Step in the Name of Love*. This is an R&B remake of the hit 1970s disco film *Saturday Night Fever*. Usher hopes to be a **producer** on this film. He is also said to be providing the **soundtrack** for an MTV film project.

Hip-hop star Eminem starred in the original version of *8 Mile* in 2002.

After 8 Mile?

Film company Miramax is said to be thinking about making an R&B version of *8 Mile*. Usher is being lined up to star in the film.

An R&B version of *Saturday Night Fever* would let Usher show off his dance moves.

And more...

Usher has also launched the Usher bank card. He has also announced his **intentions** to start up his own clothes line. Being a star may be fun, but it is certainly hard work...

producer film producers organize the people and money to make a film

Find out more

Books
Usher, Morgan Talmadge (Children's Press, 2001)
Usher: The Ultimate Entertainer, Marc S. Malkin
    (Andrews Mcmeel Publishers, 1998)

Discography
Confessions (Special Edition) (October 2004)
Confessions (March 2004)
8701 (2001)
All About U (2000)
Live (1999)
My Way (1997)
Usher (1994)

DVDs
Usher: Live Evolution 8701
Usher: U Don't Have to Call/U Got It Bad

Filmography
Dying for Dolly (2005)
Texas Rangers (2001)
Light It Up (1999)
She's All That (1999)
The Faculty (1998)

Television
Geppetto (2000)
The Bold and the Beautiful (1998)
Moesha (1997–1998)

Websites

www.kidzworld.com
This site has lots of music news and gossip.

www.laface.com
This is the website of Usher's record label, LaFace Records. Here you will find all the latest news about Usher's music releases and tours, as well as photos and features on him and other artists at the label.

www.mtv.com
Here you will get all the latest music news and reviews.

Disclaimer

Glossary

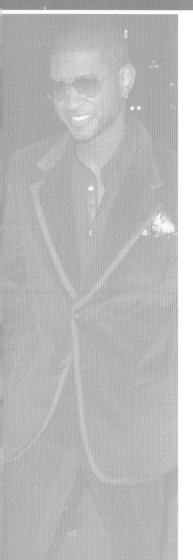

accomplishment achievement

audition interview for an actor or musician, where they show their skills

cameo when a famous person has a small part in a film or television programme

career what someone does for a job

choreographer person who makes up dance steps and teaches them to others

collaborate work together with

comparison when people see similarities between things

confessional book, film, or piece of music that tells a true personal story

credit respect

crossover artist when a star who is famous for one thing, such as music, starts to do something new, such as acting

debut first

director person in charge of making a film

executive manager in a business

feud argument or disagreement

hectic very busy

inspired take ideas from something

intentions plans

manager music managers take care of the business side of a pop star's career

medallion type of necklace

media types of communication such as television, radio, newspapers, and magazines

medley song that mixes parts of a number of songs together

Motown record label that released popular music by African-American singers in the 1960s

nominated put forward as one of the right people to win an award

producer (in film) film producers organize the people and money to make a film

producer (in music) music producers decide how a song will sound when it is being recorded

recording contract agreement between a musician and a record label to make music together

rivalry competition

rumour story that lots of people discuss, but that may not be true

sensational very exciting and impressive

soundtrack music that appears in a film

talent scout someone who looks out for talented performers such as actors, models, or athletes

tribute act that shows feelings of respect or admiration towards someone

unique different from everyone else

Index

Titles in the *Star File* series include:

Johnny Depp
Jane Bingham

Hardback   1 844 43283 1

Beyoncé Knowles
Mark Stewart

Hardback   1 844 43296 3

Jackie Chan
Dan Fox

Hardback   1 844 43295 5

Usher
Dan Whitcombe

Hardback   1 844 43298 X

David Beckham
Paul Harrison

Hardback   1 844 43297 1

Andre Benjamin
Brian Fitzgerald

Hardback   1 844 43972 0

Mary-Kate and Ashley Olsen
Stephanie Fitzgerald

Hardback   1 410 91662 6

Orlando Bloom
Kay Barnham

Hardback   1 844 43284 X

Find out about other titles in this series on our website www.raintreepublishers.co.uk